THE JOHN PHILIP KASSEBAUM COLLECTION

VOLUME ONE

65. VASE with the Arms of the Duke of Calabria
Probably Tuscany, 1470–1480

13$^{15}/_{16}$" high
See page 62

THE JOHN PHILIP KASSEBAUM COLLECTION

VOLUME ONE

Foreword by
JOHN V. G. MALLET
Keeper of the Department of Ceramics
Victoria and Albert Museum, London

THE LOWELL PRESS, INC. / KANSAS CITY
1981

FIRST EDITION
Copyright © 1981 by John Philip Kassebaum

L.C. 81-80730   ISBN 0-913504-63-7

All rights reserved. No part of this book may be reproduced,
stored in a retrieval system, or transmitted in any form or by any
means, electronic, mechanical, photocopying, recording, or otherwise,
without the prior written permission of the publisher.

Printed in the United States of America
by The Lowell Press, Inc. / Kansas City, Missouri

DEDICATION

*To the members of my family
for their love, patience and understanding.
And to the endless thousands,
who, from the dawn of history,
have taken a simple handful of clay
and formed from it
objects of utility and beauty.*

FOREWORD

Rarely are collectors of ceramics prepared to take the rough with the smooth. The smooth is 18th century Nymphenburg and Sévres, or the imperial wares of China. It walks with kings without (at its best) entirely losing the common touch. The rough comprises most slipwares, saltglaze and much tin-glazed pottery. It is often (but, with important exceptions, as we shall see) more at home in cottage and pharmacy than at court. Not all porcelain is smooth: think of 17th century Swatow. Not all pottery and stoneware is rough: remember Josiah Wedgwood. Nor can the social connotations of roughness and smoothness always be relied on: the roughest and humblest of pottery bowls have, with what looks suspiciously like inverted snobbery, been exalted by Japanese tea-masters, while the technical perfection that used to be one of the credentials of smoothness has, through industrialisation, been brought within the means of everyone. Yet broadly speaking, the categories hold, and collections can be classed as rough or smooth.

In these terms the Kassebaum Collection is rough, being comprised, essentially, of early lead- and tin-glazed earthenwares of the Mediaeval and Renaissance periods. The examples published in the present volume, the English mediaeval pottery and delftwares that are to follow it, comprise objects that appeal through vitality rather than finesse. We must not expect from most of the pieces anything approaching perfect regularity of execution. Within limits, we must accept distortion in firing, bubbling of glaze or slight running of colours, and even welcome these as adding life and variety to the pots.

It may be noticed that Mr. Kassebaum's interest in tin-glazed wares is confined to wares decorated in the so-called *grand feu* colours, which are painted onto a powdery, unfired white glaze and take their chance with it at quite high temperatures in the kiln. Not for him the more precisely controllable effects that became available to 18th century *faienciers* through the introduction of enamel colours fixed at relatively low temperatures onto a previously fired tin-glaze. Working by the earlier method, on an unfired ground, any hesitation or attempted correction will be visible on the finished piece; the method challenged painters to work with unwavering directness, and the vigour of their response can be seen on many pieces in the Kassebaum Collection.

It should not be thought that deliberation played no part in forming the wares in this collection, nor that these were objects of pure caprice like the 'funk' pottery of recent years. Most pieces owe their shapes to specific uses. Within any given workshop a high degree of standardisation in size was dictated by the size of the saggars and convenience in packing the kiln. Even in decorating ware, if a potter improvised, he usually did so within the limits of a well understood repertoire. Elaborate symmetrical patterns like that on the Talavera jars, Nos. 25 a and b, must have necessitated the laying out of the pattern by some method which has left no trace on the finished ware. A dish like No. 90, from Deruta, almost certainly had the main outlines of its painting pounced or otherwise transferred onto the pot from a drawing. It is a measure of the decorator's skill that such methods seldom seriously impair the vitality of the finished product.

When I said just now that the objects in the Kassebaum Collection must be considered as 'rough,' I was, of course, thinking of them from a 20th century standpoint. The Hispano-Moresque lustred wares of Valencia, though today they present a somewhat rough and irregular appearance, were in the 15th century objects of sufficient luxury to merit shipping from Spain to the Netherlands, Italy and still further afield. Or No. 65, an Italian drug jar, is shown by the coat of arms it bears to have been made for a personage of the most exalted rank. To its quattrocento owner, the Duke of Calabria, the jar would have appeared anything but 'rough' by comparison with other pottery known to him. The jar itself has not changed since the Duke's eye paused on it before wandering along others of the set ranged on his pharmacy shelf. Yet in the jar's new context in the Kassebaum Collection, and in the context of every other jar or container we have ever known, we perceive it differently. To be confronted with a group of pottery like that here illustrated should extend our historical imagination as well as yielding direct pleasure on our terms. Mr. Kassebaum is doing us all a service by making his collection better known.

J.V.G. MALLET

Reverse of No. 21

PREFACE and ACKNOWLEDGMENTS

This catalogue, dealing essentially with tin-glazed wares of Persia, Spain, Italy and some of Northern European manufacture, as well as lead-glazed wares of France and Germany, has been planned as the first volume of a work based upon examples selected from a collection of ceramics formed over the last twenty-three years. A second volume covering English medieval ware and English delftware is planned for a subsequent publication.

With respect to the order of entries, there has been an attempt to group objects by presumed place of production and chronological order. In the case of the Italian section the general idea has been to go from north to south as well. However, as will be evident, this plan has been modified when necessity required so as to assure, for example, that color prints would appear on pages designed to receive color impressions. Other wholly subjective deviations occur, such as the decision to insert the Faenza examples before concluding the Tuscan section with Montelupo, because that arrangement seemed to better reflect the development of the ware through the examples in the collection. The same was true in placing the Talavera or Puente dish (No. 52) next to the Mexican vases (No. 53) painted in a similar style.

Since the end of the Second World War much research has been accomplished on the origins of particular styles of Italian maiolica, including information gained through excavations at the pottery sites. For that reason it is now realized that some wares were manufactured in several localities and that some long-standing specific factory attributions should now be altered to ones of a more general nature. This practice has been undertaken here, with the result, for example, that No. 64 is now shown as Tuscan, while many similar pieces have previously been specifically attributed to the Caffaggiolo factory in Tuscany. The same situation exists in the Near-Eastern section, so that Nos. 5 and 6, sometimes called "Sultanabad," are here attributed to Persia, as their actual origination is now felt to be unknown.

At one time or another, segments of the collection have been on exhibition at the Nelson Gallery in Kansas City, Art Institute of Chicago, Wichita Art Museum, and elsewhere. Repeated reference to this in the captions would seem to serve no purpose and has been avoided. However, exhibitions have been noted when a piece was illustrated in the exhibition catalogue. Also no attempt has been made to cite, from the vast bibliographical material available, examples similar to those here illustrated. Finally, because the illustrations reflect each piece in considerable detail, the captions have not been burdened with detailed description of decoration which is clearly apparent to the eye.

The collecting of ceramics, as is true in collecting any art, comes down in large degree to a matter of personal taste. I was immediately drawn to the early more primitive forms of earthenware (sometimes designated "rough" in contradistinction to "fine" as used for 18th century faience wares and porcelains) because, to me, they better respected and followed the basic qualities of the clay from which they were formed. There is a sense of honesty and unpretentiousness about them which, in many cases, amounts to an air of sophistication, albeit perhaps unintended by the creator of the piece. With the exception of commemorative or purely decorative pieces, most wares made by medieval and Renaissance potters were intended for specific or everyday use. Consequently their products tend to give an unaffected indication of the true tastes of the day.

It is not that the more refined rococo forms seen in, say, 18th century French faience and Meissen porcelain, are not beautiful. It is rather that they appeal to me less than their earthenware predecessors, both visually and with respect to their historical importance in the development of European ceramic art. It is interesting to experience the interrelation of such development, with its recurring themes, from one area, country, or even continent, to another. Take, for example, the Persian—Spanish—Italian sequence treated hereafter, or, with more specificity, the French and English "Fecundity" dishes (Nos. 109-110). A blue-dash bordered dish was even produced in Manises (No. 50) somewhat later than its English delftware cousins of similar decoration. These and like thoughts have led me upon the present path. Along it, I have found my lead- and tin-glazed friends to be good company.

There are many people without whose assistance this volume would never have materialized. First and foremost I must acknowledge my indebtedness to my longtime and close friend, Ross E. Taggart, Senior Curator of the Nelson Gallery and Atkins Museum, Kansas City, Missouri. It was he who initially encouraged me to become a collector of ceramics. I first sought him out in the fall of 1957, after having acquired examples of English medieval ware and delftware which seemed similar to pieces in the Nelson Gallery's Burnap collection, to which I had been exposed while in school in Kansas City. Mr. Taggart had been instrumental in its formation and had published the collection catalogue. He has never failed to generously provide advice and guidance over the years since.

In connection with the preparation of this volume, he has assisted in the photography, proof-read the text, served as liaison with the publisher and, for all practical purposes, performed the responsibilities of editor, a title he has declined with characteristic modesty.

It was through Mr. Taggart that I met Joseph V. Vizcarra, Louis L. Lipski and A.J.B. Kiddell, my late good friends, to whom I am also indebted, not only for their help in the furtherance of the goals of the collection, but for their friendship and association over many years. Mr. Vizcarra, then of the Art Institute of Chicago, advised, assisted, and sometimes collaborated in my ceramic acquisitions over a period of almost twenty years. He had an excellent eye, and although his true love was English delftware, he had a keen understanding of and appreciation for Italian and Spanish tin-glazed ware and where to find it in otherwise inauspicious continental locations.

From our first meeting in 1965 until his death, Louis L. Lipski, by profession a London architect, whose fascination for and knowledge of dated and inscribed examples of English delftware is well known, actively assisted in my search in England for Spanish and Italian tin-glazed examples, as well as English delftware pieces. Over a span of seventeen years A.J.B. Kiddell, a Director of Sothebys of London and a past President of the English Ceramic Circle, alerted me to ceramic objects in oncoming sales of which he felt I should be aware, in London and elsewhere, and his evaluation and meticulous descriptions of them were of invaluable assistance.

I am deeply indebted to my friend, John V.G. Mallet, Keeper of the Department of Ceramics, Victoria and Albert Museum, who has unselfishly made available his unexcelled knowledge of Italian maiolica. In addition, I am honored that he would contribute a foreword to this volume and travel to the Ulrich Museum at Wichita State University to lecture on the occasion of the opening of the exhibition of this collection there, as a part of the proceedings in the annual conference of the National Council on Education for the Ceramic Arts.

I am indebted to the late Alice Wilson Frothingham, Curator of the Hispanic Society of America, for her courtesies and assistance in connection with the formation of the Spanish portion of the collection.

I am also indebted to Michael Archer, Deputy Keeper of the Department of Ceramics, Victoria and Albert Museum, for his expertise as to the attribution of some of the more troublesome continental wares; to Dr. Oliver Watson, Assistant Keeper of the Department of Ceramics, Victoria and Albert Museum, for his expertise relative to the classification of Near Eastern and Hispano-Moresque wares and to Timothy Husband, Curator, The Cloisters of the Metropolitan Museum of Art, New York, for his expertise with respect to the Hispano-Moresque, Catalan and lead-glazed German wares. Having said this, I must make clear the fact that all final decisions concerning the attributions which appear in the catalogue were made by me and I take full responsibility for any which, in the end, may be found inadequate.

I wish to thank Orville Crane of Kansas City for his painstaking and thorough work as photographer for this volume. I wish also to thank my good friend, Dr. Martin H. Bush, Vice President of Academic Resources of Wichita State University and Director of the Ulrich Museum of Art there, for his interest, encouragement and assistance in this project.

Finally, I wish to thank my friends and colleagues and, in particular, those who have served as Directors of the Helen Foresman Spencer Museum of Art of the University of Kansas (formerly the University of Kansas Museum of Art) during my years as Honorary Curator of Ceramics there, namely, Edward A. Maser, Director, Smart Gallery of Art, University of Chicago; Dr. Marilyn J. Stokstad, Professor of Art History, University of Kansas; A. Bret Waller, Director, Memorial Art Gallery, University of Rochester, Rochester, New York; and Charles C. Eldredge, Director, Helen Foresman Spencer Museum of Art, for their support and encouragement throughout the tenure of our association.

JOHN PHILIP KASSEBAUM
Helen Foresman Spencer Museum of Art
University of Kansas
Lawrence, Kansas

No. 28

INTRODUCTION

It has been conjectured that prehistoric man was first aware of the plastic qualities of clay from observing his own footprints in it. Later he lined the interior of a crude basket with clay to transport water. Eventually the vessel was used in conjunction with a cooking fire, and the basket exterior was burned away, producing the first low fired earthenware pot. For centuries thereafter, some neolithic pots were decorated in a design resembling the weave of a rush basket, scratched on the exterior of the vessel by using a pointed object.

Irrespective of the accurateness of this theory, it eventually became known that all clay, to varying degrees, contained water (combined chemically with other of its properties) which must be removed by firing before a vessel would permanently retain its shape. A basic form of ceramic manufacture occurred in the ancient Near East as early as the seventh millennium B.C. with the wares being baked in a slow fire covered with earth. Sometime before 4000 B.C. the vertical kiln, in which the product was elevated above the flames during firing, was in use in Persia.

While the earliest pots were made by hand, frequently through stacking coils of clay one upon the other and then smoothing or otherwise working the object into shape, the potter's wheel came into use in Mesopotamia around 3000 B.C. Earthenware was also shaped through the use of molds into which the base clay was either pressed or poured in a thick solution. Decoration was applied through the techniques of impressing and incising and the application of pigments.

The four unglazed objects illustrated in this volume ranging from an Iberian bowl, circa 300-100 B.C., thrown on the potter's wheel (No. 15); a molded and incised Hispano-Moresque wall tile, circa 14th century (No. 16); and molded Catalan ceiling (No. 39) and wall (No. 40) tiles, circa 14th to 15th century, demonstrate the strength and quiet elegance of these relatively unadorned examples of the potter's art.

In Mesopotamia, shortly after 2000 B.C., a method was perfected to render earthenware impervious to liquids, through the application of a lead-glaze, consisting of sand or other silica fused with the aid of an oxide or sulphide of lead. The technique produced a brilliant, transparent and sometimes glassy surface, usually stained yellow or brown by traces of iron in the base clay or glaze solution. The glaze could be intentionally stained a variety of colors, including green by the use of copper and brown to purple by the use of manganese. Lead-glaze was widely used thereafter by the ancient Romans, Han Dynasty Chinese and through medieval to modern times. It is exemplified here by the wares of Persia (Nos. 1 and 2), North Italy (No. 96), France (Nos. 109, 111–113), Germany (Nos. 115, 116, 118 and 119), and elsewhere.

Eventually, it was learned that the transparent lead-glaze could be turned opaque white by the addition of oxide of tin. The resulting tin-glazed ware was in use in the ancient Near East from at least 500 B.C., as is confirmed by a frieze from the Achaemenid Palace at Susa, now in the Louvre. Actually the terms "maiolica," "faience," and "delftware" all connote earthenware covered with a white tin-glaze. Its appearance was unique because it was not transparent, as in the case of lead-glaze, and left the object covered with a thick white glaze which transformed the original buff or red based clay. First in the Near East and later, during the High Renaissance, in Spain and Italy, this ware attained great importance and popularity by reason of its extraordinary receptiveness to painted decoration, and the extremely high quality of the decoration painted upon it.

In all early tin-glazed wares, the base clay was first shaped and fired to an absorbent biscuit, which was then dipped into, or brushed with, the solution of tin-glaze, and dried. Painting was then done on the absorbent surface of the unfired glaze with a palette of enamels derived from various metallic oxides, including purple and brown from manganese, green from copper, blue from cobalt, yellow from antimony, and red and orange from iron oxide. Because the enamel was immediately absorbed into the surface it was necessary that the design be painted rapidly and with dexterity as it was impossible to rectify mistakes. Once the enamel was applied the piece was fired again at the higher temperature of the *grand feu,* in which enamel and white base were fused into a vitreous, permanently colored mass. In some examples, a second covering of clear lead-glaze was then added over the tin-glaze.

At its best, maiolica painting merges with the plasticity of the ware to reach a force and excellence only attainable in the ceramic milieu. It is, after all, a ceramic art form in which absolute fidelity to the properties of clay is required. With its imperishable color, this ware reflects the true grandeur of the High Renaissance in Italy. The great bulk of the collection is comprised of examples of tin-glazed ware which are intended to trace the development and spread of its manufacture from Persia to Spain, Italy, Continental Europe and England (the latter of which lies outside the scope of the present volume).

Sometimes a covering of metallic luster was applied over the tin-glazed enamel decoration, providing a different and striking dimension to the ware. Silver was used for the pale yellow tones and copper for the darker hues. The luster solution was painted on the tin-glazed ware after the initial firing. A final firing took place in a low temperature "reduction" kiln which reduced the oxides to the metallic state. The piece emerged from the kiln blackened by soot and smoke but, after being rubbed with a cloth, the decorated parts appeared as metallic silver, copper or gold.

Although, as we have seen, ceramic manufacture flourished in the Near East from the earliest time, it was in the 9th century, stimulated by the importation of Chinese T'ang ware, and through the support and encouragement of the Abbasid Caliphs in Mesopotamia, that glazed wares of some interest were produced there in imitation of the Chinese. Of note is a lead-glazed splashed or mottled ware in which the red body of the piece was covered with white slip, or liquid mixture of clay and water, over which was applied a yellowish, transparent lead-glaze. In order to lessen the danger of the decoration running in the kiln it was executed in thick wide lines (No. 2).

The sgraffiato technique was also successfully used, where the body of the piece was covered with a transparent or yellowish toned lead glaze, through which an incised decoration was scratched with a metal or wooden instrument (No. 1). Frequently, to enhance the contrast, the buff body of the ware was dipped, after its first "biscuit" firing, into a solution of white slip. The lines of decoration were scratched through the slip and into the body, to be followed by an application of transparent lead-glaze and an additional firing. The design could be sharpened by underglaze pigments of copper, cobalt, manganese or antimony. Many variations exist, and it was widely produced (Nos. 14 and 97).

However, it was in the area of the manufacture of tin-glazed ware and its development through the 15th century that the greatest debt is owed the Muslim potters of the Near East. The forms were extremely varied and ranged from dishes, convex-sided bowls and tiles to drug vessels of considerable style. Examples with strong green glazes bearing a design in black were executed in profusion in Persia in the 13th and 14th centuries (Nos. 4, 5, and 8). Lusterware of high quality had also been developed (Nos. 7, 9–13). It is interesting to note the variations in form of the waisted albarelli, or dry drug jars, produced from the 13th to 15th centuries (Nos. 3, 6, 7 and 8).

It was tin-glazed ware such as this that flew on the wings of the Muslim expansion through the Near East, across North Africa, and into southern Spain. As would be expected, it had a significant impact on local ceramic production. By the second quarter of the 15th century, the artistic leadership in European pottery manufacture was centered at Manises in Valencia (Nos. 17 and 18). Powerfully executed, the dramatic Hispano-Moresque lustered ware was of quality and interest long after the zenith of its manufacture in the 15th century (Nos. 19–24).

Spanish craftsmen also excelled in the production of non-lustered tin-glazed ware, the most important center of which was Talavera de la Reina in Castile. This factory, which was active from the early part of the 16th century, was initially heavily influenced by the Italian and Flemish potters employed there. In the 16th century, wares of considerable distinction were made in the forms of gallipots, albarelli and various large vases.

Some of the most important early Talavera wares were made for the enormous pharmacy in the Royal Monastery of San Lorenzo del Escorial, which was built by Philip II to celebrate Spain's victory over the French at Saint-Quentin on August 10, 1557. That date happens to be the feast day of Saint Lawrence, a third century martyr, who was roasted to death on a gridiron. According to popular tradition, the Escorial itself takes its shape from Saint Lawrence's emblem being laid out as a vast grid of intersecting corridors and courtyards. So too, is the grid motif reflected in the arms of the Escorial as evidenced by the gallipots and jars in the collection (Nos. 25–27). By the 18th century Talavera potters were making personalized items for use at the monastery's table, such as the cruet set made for Friar Bernardo de Lorca (No. 28).

Talavera also produced large covered jars with spirited scenes of hunting, falconry, and animals painted on the sides, which date from the late 16th through the 17th century (No. 29). All manner of quality tin-glazed ware was produced ranging even to the smallest paving and wall tiles (Nos. 34–38).

During this time, tin-glazed ware was also manufactured in the neighboring center of Puente del Arzobispo. Frequently, these products are virtually indistinguishable from those of Talavera (Nos. 30 and 52). In the later 17th and 18th centuries a much bolder ware was produced there, frequently decorated with drawings of animals, trees, architectural motifs and birds. While it is true that this later production lost some of its original refinement, it partly made up for it in the vigor of the execution of the decoration (Nos. 31–33).

A vast amount of product from the Talavera area factories, in virtually every form imaginable, was exported throughout the world. In the 17th and 18th centuries, Talavera potters migrated to Mexico and established a successful ceramic industry there (No. 53).

Earthenware of considerable merit was also manfactured in Catalonia, where, during the 14th and 15th centuries, ceiling and wall tiles of an austere Gothic quality were produced (Nos. 39 and 40). Under the influence of the wares of Valencia a series of well formed albarelli appeared in the latter part of the 15th century in a style reminiscent of the Hispano-Moresque (Nos. 41 and 42). At their best they exhibit form and decoration highly compatible with Italian examples contemporary to them (No. 43). In the 17th and 18th centuries a series of blue and white dishes was produced there decorated with sailing vessels, architectural motifs, animals and figures, highlighted by a strong blackish-blue glaze (Nos. 44–46).

While it is clear that wares of distinction and quality were produced in Spain, of equal importance is the great influence exerted by the Spanish wares upon the Italian potters of the early Renaissance.

The earliest Italian tin-glaze is generally ascribed to the 14th century, where, in the vicinity of Florence, examples decorated in manganese and copper green were manufactured. It followed a widespread Mediterranean style typified by the Spanish wares of Teruel (No. 47). The exact factory sites are unknown, but examples of their products have been found in abandoned medieval wells in Orvieto, in Umbria, and the name "Orvieto" has generally been given it (although other examples are known in other sites in Umbria and Lazio). The decoration is clearly Gothic, reflects Mediterranean influence, and frequently features heraldic shields, birds, plants, fish and geometric ornamentation (Nos. 54–61).

In the last quarter of the quattrocento in Italy, the High Renaissance was a time for exploring new ideas and devising new techniques. The art of painting flourished there and had attained an advanced state of refinement. Even small centers had schools of painting and craftsmanship, supported and channelled by the church and local nobility.

Ancient classical literature was being rediscovered and interest was revived in Greek and Roman art. It was natural that classical forms should influence not only the architecture and painting of the day, but ceramic design as well. It was from this background that the maiolica masterpieces of the 15th and early 16th centuries were produced.

By the 15th century, Hispano-Moresque ware was imported into Italy through Pisa, the principal port of Tuscany, via the island of Majorca. Through this association, and the belief that the wares were made at the latter locality, the term "maiolica," a corruption of Majorca, was given to the imported luster ware. By the 16th century "Maiolica" became a term in Italy for all tin-glazed earthenware of the Renaissance period, whether lustered or not.

The imported Hispano-Moresque ware had an immediate effect upon the local ceramic manufacture in Tuscany, which was, by that time, the most important in Italy. It was there in the second quarter of the 15th century that the famous Tuscan "oak leaf" ware was manufactured, usually with thick dark blue decoration and painting reflecting an abstract power and freedom, showing Spanish influence in the stylized oak leaf foliage with which they were decorated (No. 62).

In the third quarter of the 15th century maiolica manufacture in Italy came into its own. This so-called "Gothic period" lasted through the end of the century and produced in Tuscany, Faenza and elsewhere some of the masterpieces of European ceramic art. The ware was both decorative and utilitarian and featured magnificent albarelli and drug vases made for the greatest families in the land.

One of the most popular decorative themes was that of "Gothic Foliage," or "Gothic Scroll," possibly suggested by illuminations from contemporary choir books. The drawing is stark and masculine, executed in simple colors often dominated by somber dark blue and illuminated by a superb orange-yellow and clear green (No. 65 frontispiece).

In the 15th and 16th centuries, Tuscan wares were made in a great variety of forms throughout their several centers of manufacture (Nos. 63, 64, 66, 67 and 71). Although Siena was a site of ceramic manufacture for centuries, some of the earliest examples of maiolica definitely attributable to Siena are a series of paving tiles made for the Petrucci Palace in 1509 (Nos. 68–70).

Creative excellence was not to be monopolized in Tuscany, however. From about the third quarter of the 15th century through the early 17th century, wares of great style and appeal were produced at Faenza in Emilia. From the last quarter of the 15th century through 1530 they were equal in quality to that of any other center of Italian manufacture. Drug jars of pleasing shape and decoration, bearing in Gothic script the names of the drugs and unguents, were made during this time (Nos. 72–75). Then and later, molded wares were produced (Nos. 76 and 77) as were tazzas and latticed bowls (Nos. 78 and 79) in which the principal decoration was the brilliant white glaze, much of it exported as "Bianchi d' Faenza."

Faenza wares are known for the excellent proportion of their form, the power of drawing and the quality of color. Great quantities were exported abroad with the result that tin-glazed earthenware of several continental countries is now called "faience" in its honor.

The potteries in Montelupo had produced some of the fine Tuscan wares of the 15th century and by the end of the 16th century were still making wares of utility and interest (Nos. 81 and 82). In the 17th century a series of brilliantly colored dishes appeared, often decorated with stylized figures, designed to attract a larger contemporary patronage (No. 80).

A second great period of Italian maiolica manufacture extended from 1500 to about 1530, during which the more primitive thrust of the "Gothic" period was softened and refined. The "Istoriato" or pictorial manner of maiolica decoration commenced in the early 16th century in the factories of Castel Durante and Urbino situated within the Duchy of Urbino. The finest work in this area is considered that of Nicola of Urbino, whose sensitive brushwork and deft use of color place him in the forefront of maiolica painters (No. 87). Completed through the tin-glazed stage, frequently the piece would be taken to the neighboring factory of Gubbio, also situated in the Duchy of Urbino, for the addition of the famous Gubbio luster with its rich ruby hues (No. 84).

It was at the Umbrian factory of Deruta during the first quarter of the 16th century that the great iridescent luster, with its moonlight tones, was perfected (No. 90). Emulating the lusterwares of Valencia (cf. Nos. 18 and 92), the artisans of Deruta were the first to totally master this technique in Italy. Enjoying great popularity, the wares were decorated in religious (No. 89) and other motifs and were frequently painted in a palette of tawny orange, yellow, blue and manganese (No. 91).

In the 16th century the workshops of Venice produced wares known for a glaze stained with cobalt blue to a pale grayish or lavender color, upon which designs in dark blue, white and manganese were particularly effective (Nos. 93 and 94). In the late 17th and early 18th centuries, molded wares of interesting detail were executed in the neighboring factory of Angarano (No. 95).

Also, chiefly in Northern Italy, quality sgraffiato ware was produced (Nos. 96 and 97).

In the 17th and 18th centuries the Istoriato style was revived in the southern factory of Castelli, near Naples. There, pictorial decorations were painted in muted colors and represented a last resurgence of the art of Italian maiolica (No. 98).

Other works of interest were being produced in southern Italy in the 17th century (No. 101). An amusing series of figures was executed in the workshop of Cerreto Sannita in the 18th century (Nos. 102–103). But by the end of the century the vitality and vibrance of the wares of the High Renaissance were but a distant memory (No. 104).

Maiolica, in an imitation of the style of Castel Durante, was produced in Sicily in the late 16th through 18th centuries (No. 105). Of somewhat unique design is a form of albarello with an unusually pronounced waist, made, among other places, in the workshops of Palermo and Trapani (Nos. 106–108).

In the meantime, in France, during the mid-16th century, relief-decorated lead-glazed wares of Bernard Palissy came into high vogue as the "style rustique." Much Palissy work consists of molded models of natural objects such as plants, lizards and fish (No. 111) and was influenced by silver and other metal forms. One of the most notable of his subjects is "La Fecundity" (No. 109) which was directly responsible for the design of a series of large dishes in English delftware manufactured over 100 years later (No. 110). A quantity of lead-glazed ware was also produced in Avignon (No. 113).

Lead-glazed relief decorated earthenware was also popular in the 15th and 16th centuries in Germany and the Tirol. Frequently denominated "Hafner" ware, it is strong, forceful and of a direct medieval derivation stemming from the art of the master tile makers of the area. It can be sumptuous in color and typifies the German Renaissance in its primitive, strong Gothic overtones (Nos. 115–117), as well as in its form of highest sensitivity (No. 118). Rhenish lead-glazed ware was also produced in the 16th century with significant charm and appeal (No. 119, which was apparently made for the English market).

Italian maiolica continued to be prized and much in demand in areas far from Italy. In the 16th century the manufacture of tin-glaze ware spread north across the continent, and Italian potters established workshops in various locations, including sites in France, Germany, Switzerland and the Netherlands. The collection contains examples of 18th century French (No. 114) and Swiss (No. 125) manufacture.

The early Netherlandish pieces show a direct Italian influence (No. 120). But 17th and 18th century examples, executed after Holland and the other six provinces of the northern Netherlands had secured their independence in 1609, evidence a form and decorative design, frequently influenced by Chinese export ware, and were more removed from their earlier models (Nos. 122 and 123). Closer to traditional style and decoration, the tile of the Madonna (No. 124) is probably of Portuguese attribution.

Tin-glazed ware crossed the English Channel from the Netherlands in the 16th century where it made a striking contrast to the brown and green lead-glazed wares then prevalent. Some of the most appealing of all tin-glazed pottery was produced subsequently in England, which, together with English medieval ware, will be the subject of Volume Two of this catalogue.

J.P.K.

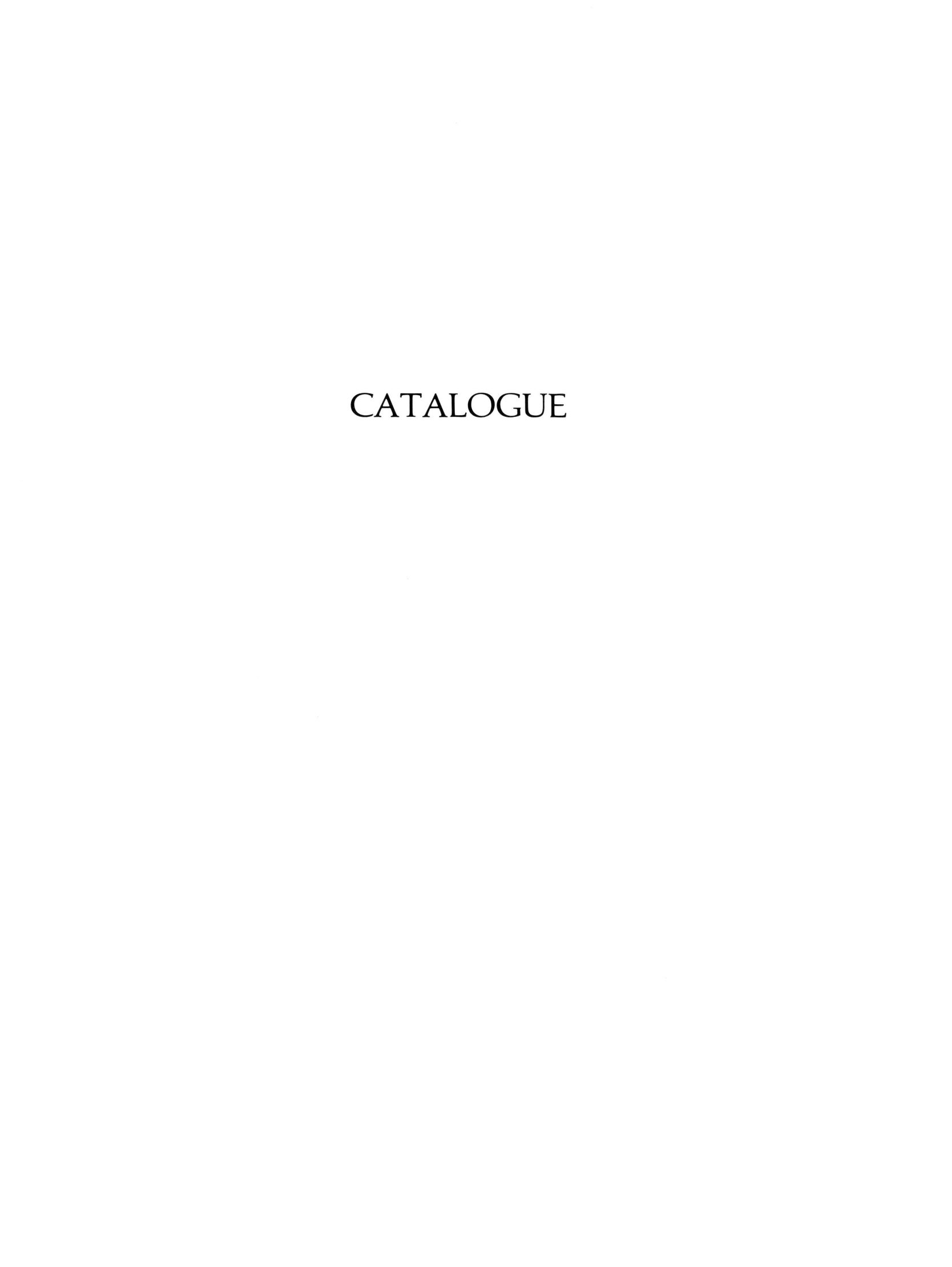

CATALOGUE

1. BOWL with sgraffiato designs
Persia, 11th–12th century

Interior lead glazed; incised slip; background cream, design in reddish-brown, rim green stain
2⅞" high; 6⅜" diameter
Ex collection Buckingham, Chicago

NEAR EAST

2. FOOTED DISH
Persia, 10th–11th century
Sari ware

Slip decoration
7¾" diameter
Cf. Robert J. Charleston, ed., *World Ceramics*, 1968, plate 210, p. 78

3. ALBARELLO 4 11/16″ high
Persia, 13th century Ex collection Brocksom, London

4. JAR
Persia, 13th–14th century
Dark green glaze; design in black
9¼" high

5. FOUR-HANDLED JAR   Blue-green glaze; design in black
Persia, 13th–14th century   5" high; 6⅞" greatest diameter

6. ALBARELLO Incandescence from burial
Persia or Syria 5½" high
13th century

7. ALBARELLO Luster decoration
Probably Persia, 5⅝" high
15th–16th century

8. ALBARELLO
Persia, 13th century

Cream-colored ground; horizontal stripes and geometric patterns in black; vertical stripes in blue
Incandescence from burial
6⅛" high

9, 10, 11, 12. FOUR TILES
Persia, early 14th–15th century

Lustered
Base glaze white with brown background (lightly lustered) developing design in reserve; light blue outlines and accents
6⅜" greatest width

13. TILE
Persia, 15th–16th century

Base glaze white with light orange (lightly lustered) background developing design in reserve and border inscription in *naskhi*; outlines in blue
12¼" x 8¾"

14. **FOOTED BOWL**

Cyprus or Syria,
12th–13th century

Crusader ware
Interior with cream-colored glaze, sgraffiato lines; splotches of yellow and green
3⅛" high; 5⅞" diameter

15. BOWL
Iberia (?), 300–100 B.C.

Unglazed buff-colored clay with designs in black
5" diameter
Ex collection Joseph V. Vizcarra, Lombard, Illinois

SPAIN

16. **TILE**
Hispano-Moresque, *circa* 14th century

Unglazed
11" x 19"
Thuluth script meaning "There is no conqueror but God"—The motto of the Nasrid kings of Granada. Similar examples exist in the Alhambra in Granada

17. ALBARELLO
Hispano-Moresque;
Manises (Valencia),
mid-15th century

Lustered
11 11/16" high

20. DISH
Hispano-Moresque; Manises (Valencia),
16th century

15⅜" diameter
Ex collection Joseph V. Vizcarra,
Lombard, Illinois

21. DISH
Hispano-Moresque; Manises (Valencia), 16th century

White ground with design in copper luster; painted convex center
14¾" diameter

22. DISH
Hispano-Moresque, Valencia with Catalan influences
16th century

White ground with design in copper luster
15" diameter

23. FOUR-HANDLED BOWL

Hispano-Moresque; Manises (Valencia), 16th century

White ground with design in copper luster
9" greatest width (across handles)

24. HONEY JAR
Hispano-Moresque;
Manises (Valencia),
17th–18th century

White ground with design
in copper luster
9½" high

25 A-B. PAIR OF DRUG JARS (gallipots)

Talavera de la Reina (Castile), third quarter of 16th century

11½" high
With the Arms of the Royal Monastery of San Lorenzo del Escorial bearing the grid of St. Lawrence and the lion of the Hieronymite Order
Ex collection Boix, Madrid

Illustrated in *Talavera Pottery* by Alice Wilson Frothingham, fig. 10, p. 14, where an attribution to Juan Flores is suggested. Flores had been summoned from Flanders to El Escorial to become Philip II's master tile painter in 1563 (p. 15).
Also in *Tile Panels of Spain 1500–1600*, Mrs. Frothingham writes that similar jars decorated with strapwork, terms and foliage in the Flemish manner, together with heraldic shields bearing the grid of St. Lawrence and the lion of the Hieronymite Order may well have come from the hand of the workshop of Juan Fernandez (p. 54).

Illustrated in *The Triumph of Humanism; Exhibition of the Decorative Arts of the Renaissance*, California Palace of the Legion of Honor, San Francisco, 1977, fig. 93.

26 A-B. PAIR OF DRUG JARS

Talavera de la Reina (Castile), last quarter of the 16th century

11⅞" high
With the Arms of the Royal Monastery of San Lorenzo del Escorial
Ex collection Boix, Madrid
The end papers were adapted from the design of these jars

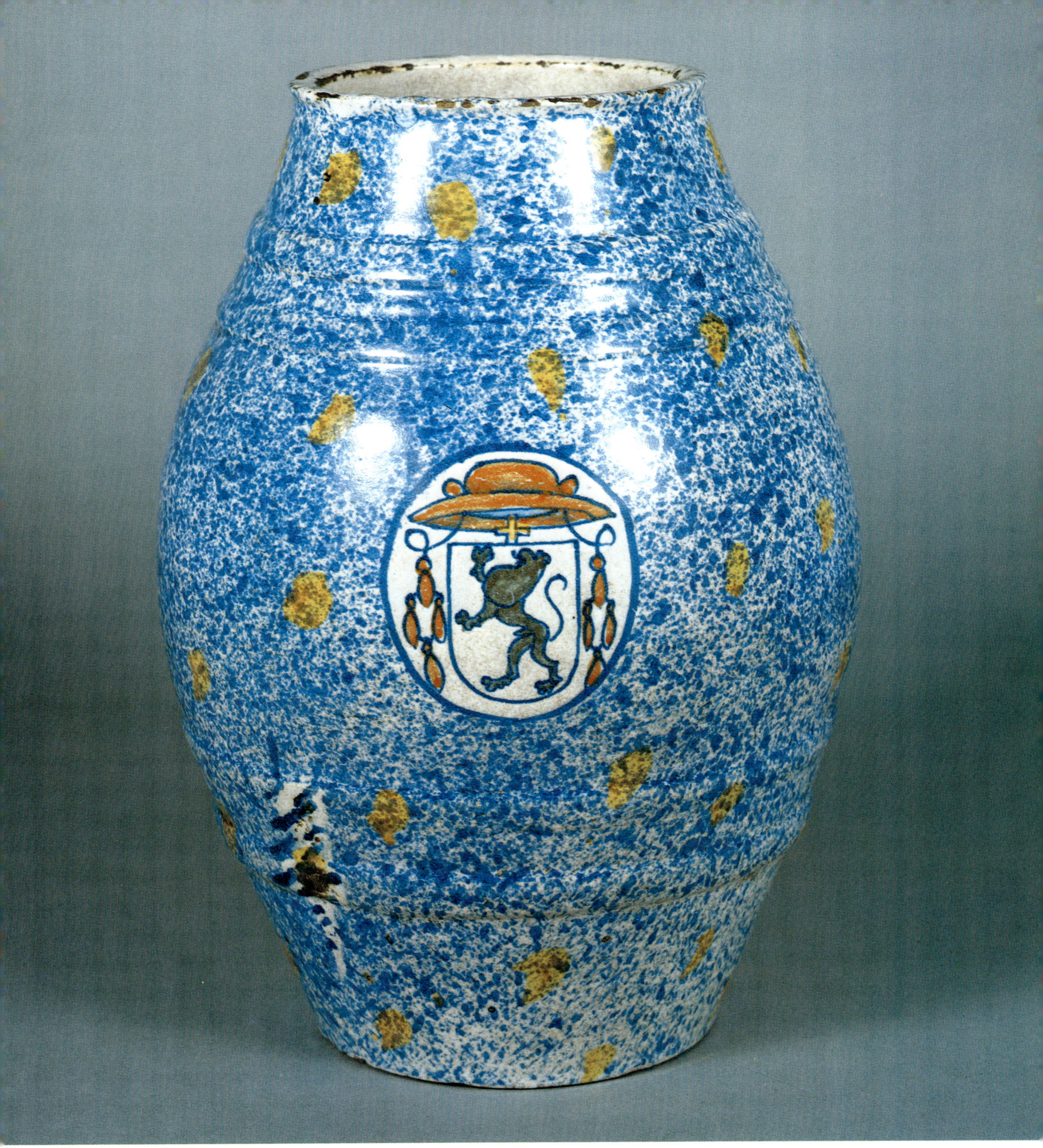

27. DRUG JAR
Talavera de la Reina (Castile), last quarter of 16th century

10⅝" high
With the Arms of the Royal Monastery of San Lorenzo del Escorial

Inscribed: DiA PRVNvS (Made from dried plums)
Ex collection Joseph V. Vizcarra, Lombard, Illinois

28. **CRUET SET**
Talavera de la Reina
(Castile), 1768–1773

Tray, 7⅝″ x 10½″; each cruet 5″ high
With the Arms of the Royal Monastery of San
Lorenzo del Escorial; tray inscribed with the name of
Friar Bernardo de Lorca (in the Escorial from 1768–1773)
Ex collection Joseph V. Vizcarra, Lombard, Illinois

29. TWO-HANDLED VASE   17" high (without base)

Talavera de la Reina (Castile), early 17th century

29

30. DEEP DISH 13" diameter
Talavera de la Reina
or Puente del Arzobispo
(Castile), 17th century

31. BOWL   4¾" high; 9⅜" diameter
Puente del Arzobispo
(Castile), 18th century

32. BOWL
Puente del Arzobispo
(Castile), 18th century

White ground with design in yellow, blue, orange, green, and manganese (Coloring similar to No. 31)
5⅝" high; 9¾" diameter

33. BOWL
Puente del Arzobispo (Castile), 18th century

White ground with design in yellow, blue, orange, green, and manganese
(Coloring similar to No. 31)
5⅝" high; 10⅛" diameter

34. TILE (center)　　White ground with designs in blue
Talavera de la Reina　4⅜" square
(Castile), 15th century

35 A-D.　TILES　　White ground with designs in blue
Talavera de la Reina　Each 3½" square
(Castile), 15th century

36, 37, 38. THREE TILES
Talavera de la Reina (Castile), 17th–18th century

White ground with designs in blue, green, yellow, and orange
Each 2⅝" x 5⅜"

39. **TILE**
(Fantastic Leaf Man)
Barcelona (Catalonia),
14th–15th century

Unglazed
16¼″ x 15¾″
Ex collection Oscar Bundy, Vienna
Cf. *Cerámica Catalana Decorada*, Barcelona, 1974, plate 4A. Andreu Batllori y Munné and L. M. Llubià y Munné attribute a similar tile to Catalonia. See also *Cerámica Catalana* by d'Alexandre Cirici, Barcelona, 1977, page 171

40. HOUSE TILE Unglazed, buff-colored clay
Catalonia, 14th–15th century 10⅜" × 10¾"

41. ALBARELLO

Catalonia, 15th century

12⅝" high
Cf. Dr. J. Chompret, *Faiences Francàises Primitives*, Paris, 1946, where a similar example is illustrated at fig. 239 and attributed to Narbonne

42. ALBARELLO
Catalonia, 16th century

Lustered
12½" high

43. ALBARELLO
Catalonia, 15th century

White ground with design in blue
11½" high

44. DISH
Catalonia, 17th–18th century

White ground with design in blue
8″ diameter
Ex collection Joseph V. Vizcarra,
Lombard, Illinois

45. DISH
Catalonia, 18th century

White ground with design in blue
8¼" diameter
Ex collection Joseph V. Vizcarra,
Lombard, Illinois

46. DISH
Catalonia, 18th century

White ground with blue design
14½" diameter
Ex collection Joseph V. Vizcarra,
Lombard, Illinois

47. MORTAR
Teruel (Aragon)
15th–16th century

White ground with designs in green and manganese
5" high

48. ALBARELLO Deep blue glaze
Probably Catalonia 7⅞" high
17th–18th century

49. ALBARELLO
Probably Valencia, but similar examples have been attributed to Seville (Andalusia), late 17th century

White ground with design in blue, green, manganese, and yellow
9⅝" high

50. BOWL
Manises (Valencia),
late 18th century

White ground with design in blue, yellow, green, orange, and brown (probably manganese)
10¾" diameter

51. ALBARELLO
Probably Valencia,
late 18th century

White ground spattered with blue
7" high
Ex collection Joseph V. Vizcarra,
Lombard, Illinois

52. DISH
Talavera de la Reina or
Puente del Arzobispo
(Castile), 18th century

White ground with blue design
12⅛" diameter
Ex collection Joseph V. Vizcarra,
Lombard, Illinois

53. PAIR OF VASES
Mexico, 18th century

White ground with design in blue
7½" high
Probably made by artisans from
Talavera de la Reina

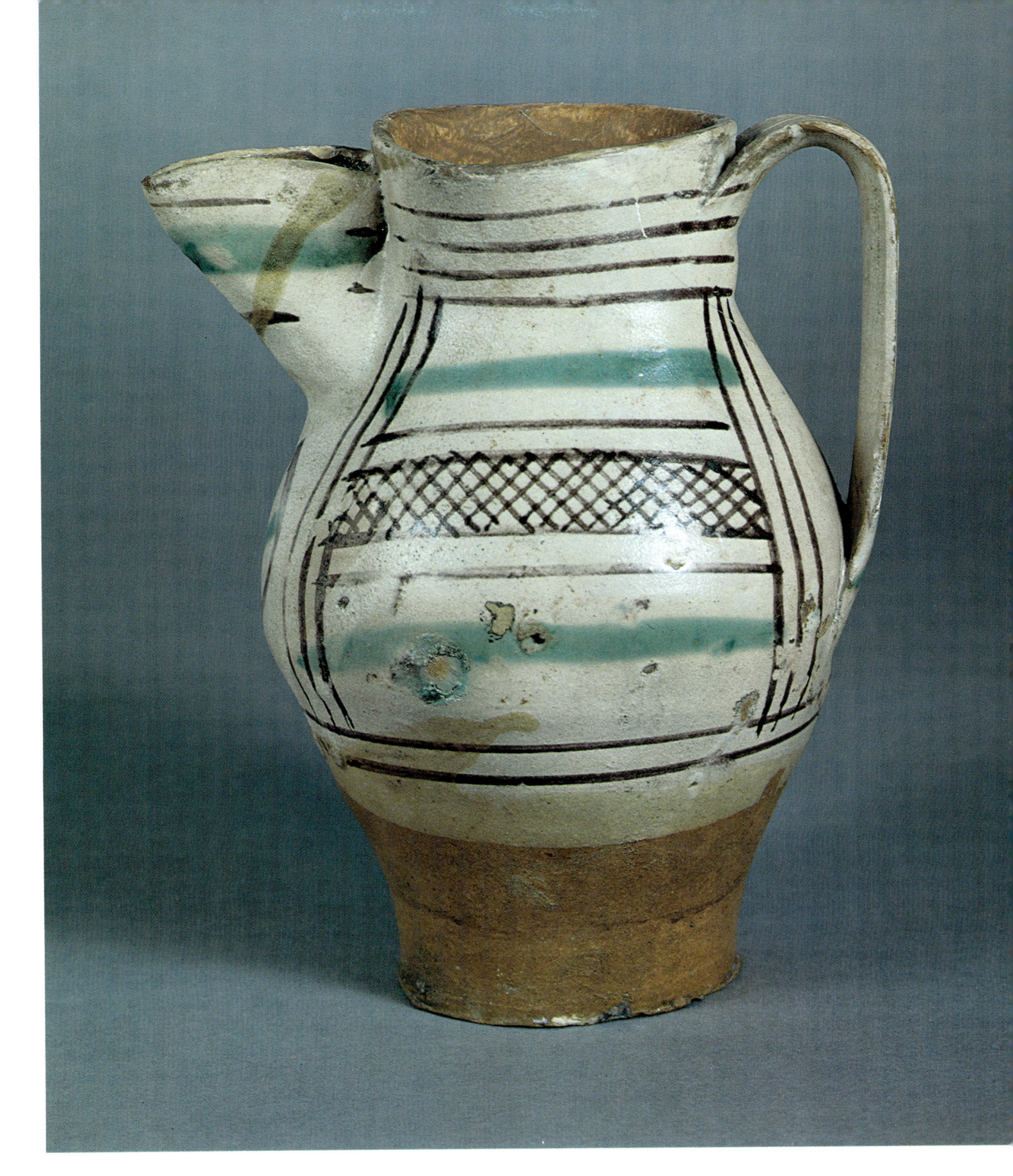

54. JUG
Orvieto (Umbria),
14th century

6¾" high
Illustrated: *Antiques*,
Feb., 1967, p. 202, fig. 1
Ex collections Imbert, Rome;
William Ridout, London and Toronto

ITALY

55. **BOWL WITH HANDLES**

Orvieto (Umbria), late 14th or early 15th century

Cream-colored ground with design in green and manganese
9 15/16" diameter; 11 5/8" with handles
Ex collections Imbert, Rome; William Ridout, London and Toronto

56. BOWL WITH HANDLES
Umbria or Lazio, 14th century

Cream-colored ground with design in green and manganese
10⁷⁄₁₆" diameter; 11¼" with handles

57. BOWL
Umbria or Lazio, 14th century

Cream-colored ground with design in green and manganese
9⅝" diameter

58. DISH
Orvieto (Umbria),
14th century

Cream-colored
8 3/16" diameter
Ex collections Imbert, Rome;
William Ridout, London and Toronto

59. BOWL
Orvieto (Umbria), late 14th or early 15th century

Cream-colored ground with design in green and manganese
5¼" diameter
Illustrated: *Antiques*, Feb., 1967, p. 202, fig. 1
Ex collections Imbert, Rome; William Ridout, London and Toronto

60. BOWL
Orvieto (Umbria),
14th century

Cream-colored ground with design
in green and manganese
4¾" diameter
Illustrated: *Antiques*,
Feb., 1967, p. 202, fig. 1
Ex collections Imbert, Rome;
William Ridout, London and Toronto

61. JUG
Umbria, possibly Orvieto,
early 15th century

15⅞" high
Ex collections Imbert, Rome,
Thomas Harris, London

62. DEEP DISH
Florentine zone, perhaps Bacchereto (Tuscany), second quarter of 15th century

10″ diameter
Galeazzo Cora, *Storia della Maiolica di Firenze e del Contado*, Florence, 1973, plate 109a shows two border fragments from Bacchereto with a similar pattern
Illustrated: Frida Schottmuller, *Furniture and Interior Decoration of the Italian Renaissance*, New York, 1921, plate 56.
Ex collection Pallazzo Davanzati, Florence

63. ALBARELLO
Tuscany, 15th century

Cream-colored ground with designs in blue and orange
7⅝" high
Illustrated: *Antiques*, Feb., 1967, p. 203, fig. 4

64. ALBARELLO
Tuscany, late 15th
or early 16th century

White ground with designs in blue,
green, yellow, and orange
10⅞" high

65. VASE with the Arms of the Duke of Calabria

Tuscany or South Italy, 1470-1480

13 5/16" high; 10 11/16" at widest point
From the Aragonese set of which other examples are illustrated by Guido Donatone in *Maioliche Napoletani della Speziera Aragonese di Castelnuovo*, Naples, 1970 (There attributed to Naples)

See also Tavole VI(a) *Faenza Bollettino del Museo Internazionale delle Ceramiche in Faenza*, 1974 and J.V.G. Mallet's article, *"Some Maiolicas from Faenza in English Collections."*

Illustrated: *Antiques,* Feb., 1967, p. 203, fig. 2
See also frontispiece

66. PLAQUE
Tuscany, 16th century

White ground with linear designs in blue; central medallion in yellow and orange in Renaissance knot design
11¾" x 10⅛"

67. SPOUTED SYRUP JAR

Tuscany, first half
of 16th century

9⅝" high
Inscribed: SY. D. BRETONICA (possibly *Betonica*. If so, syrup of wood Betony)

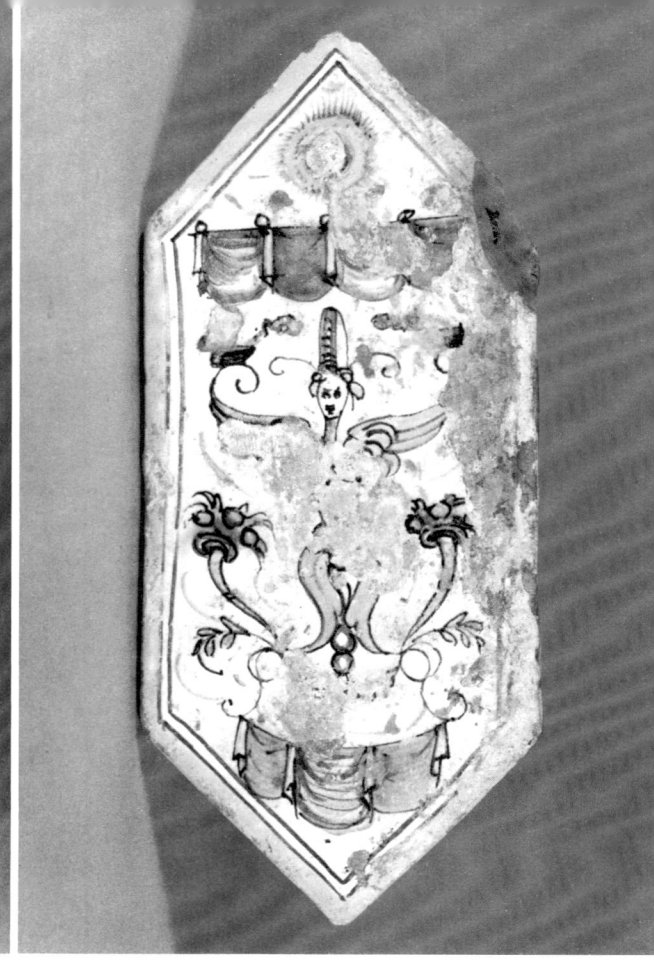

68. FLOOR TILE
Siena (Tuscany), *circa* 1509

Yellow background over white base glaze with design in yellow, blue, green, and rust
7½" x 7½"
From the Petrucci Palace, Siena
Cf. Bernard Rackham, Victoria and Albert Museum, *Catalogue of Italian Maiolica,* Vol. II, London, 1940, plate 62, No. 386a

69. FLOOR TILE
Tuscany, *circa* 1600

White ground with design in yellow, green and blue
7½" x 3¼"
From the Petrucci Palace, Siena. Probably made at Pantaneto, Siena, by Maestro Girolamo di Marco in 1600 as part of restorations to the earlier set of tiles made for the same palace.
Cf. Bernard Rackham, Victoria and Albert Museum, *Catalogue of Italian Maiolica,* Vol. II, London, 1940, plate 154, No. 955

70. **FLOOR TILE**
Siena (Tuscany), *circa* 1509

Dark blue-black ground over glaze with design in yellow, green, and orange
8" x 5½"
From the Petrucci Palace, Siena
Cf. Bernard Rackham, Victoria and Albert Museum, *Catalogue of Italian Maiolica*, Vol. II, London, 1940, plate 62, No. 386a

71. JAR with the Arms 11½" high; 9¼" greatest width
of the Medici
Tuscany, late 16th or
early 17th century

72. SPOUTED SYRUP JAR
Faenza (Emilia), 1460–1470

White ground with design in blue
8" high
Inscribed: Miel Violadi (honey of violets)
Illustrated: *Antiques*, Feb., 1967, p. 202, fig. 2
Ex collection Hall

73. UNGUENT JAR
Faenza (Emilia), last quarter
of 15th century

7" high
Inscribed: V. aureu (golden ointment)

74. DRY DRUG JAR
Faenza (Emilia), last quarter
of 15th century

3⅝" high
Inscribed: Senna p. (senna or cassia powder)
Illustrated: *Antiques*, Feb., 1967, p. 202, fig. 2

75. UNGUENT JAR
Faenza (Emilia), last quarter of 15th century

6⅜" high
Inscribed: V. rosato (rose-water ointment)

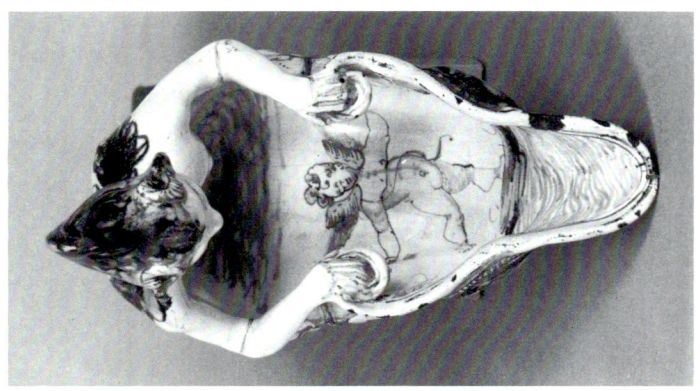

76. **WATER SCOOP**
Faenza (Emilia) or
Deruta (Umbria),
early 17th century

7¼" high; 7⁹⁄₁₆" greatest length

77. EWER
Faenza (Emilia), 1639

11⅝" high
Made for the wedding of Andrea Corsini and Agnotetta de' Medici, February 2, 1639
See Luigi Passerini, *Genealogia e Storia della Famiglia Corsini*, Firenze, 1858, Tav. XIV
Illustrated: *Antiques*, Feb., 1967, p. 206, fig. 11

78. MOLDED TAZZA
Faenza (Emilia) or Deruta (Umbria), early 17th century

White ground with design in black, blue, green, yellow, and orange
9½" diameter

79. LATTICED BOWL
Faenza (Emilia),
late 16th–early 17th century

White ground with design
in blue and orange
10⅜" diameter

80. DISH with design of striding dragoon
Montelupo (Tuscany), early 17th century

13⅛" diameter
Illustrated: *Antiques*, Feb., 1967, p. 206, fig. 12

81. SPOUTED SYRUP JAR
Montelupo (Tuscany),
late 16th or early 17th century

White ground with design in blue, accents in orange and green
9⅜" high
Inscribed: SY.D.S. RADICE (syrup of fennel and parsley)
Illustrated: *Antiques*, Feb., 1967, p. 205, fig. 8

82. **SPOUTED SYRUP JAR**
Montelupo (Tuscany),
late 16th or early 17th century

White ground with design in blue, orange, green, and brown
9 1/16" high
Inscribed: SY. DI. INDIVIA (syrup of endive)

83. **SPOUTED SYRUP JAR**
Probably Duchy of Urbino or Deruta (Umbria), *circa* 1530

Lustered
9½" high
Inscribed: OXIMEL . Q (syrup of clarified honey and vinegar) Q may refer to *Quercus*, implying the use of oak bark, buds, leaves and acorns
Illustrated: *Antiques*, Feb., 1967, p. 205, fig. 9

84. DISH with design of the Roman Emperor Gaius Mucius Scaevola placing his hand in the fire before his enemy, the Etrurian monarch Porsenna, indicating his disregard of fear at the threat of being tortured by him

Urbino, lustered at Gubbio (Urbino) in the style of Nicola of Urbino, dated 15-6 (1536)

9⅜" diameter
Ex collection H. O. Havemeyer

85. DISH with design
of piping shepherd
Urbino, possibly Patanazzi workshop,
late 16th–early 17th century

White ground with design in
orange, green, brown, and blue
9¾" diameter
Illustrated: *Antiques*, Feb., 1967, p. 205, fig. 10
Ex collection Clement Ingleby

86. PLAQUE with design of the penitent St. Jerome
Urbino, dated 1658

White ground with design in blue, green, manganese, and orange
9¾" x 7¼"
Inscribed P.P.M.F. 1658
(Pietro Paolo Mancini?)

87. DISH with design of "Cyrus Medes"
Castel Durante (Urbino) or Urbino, about 1525

8½" diameter
One of a type frequently attributed to Nicola of Urbino

88. DRUG BOTTLE
Northeast Italy, probably Castel Durante (Urbino), mid–16th century

White ground with design in blue, green, and yellow
9" high
Inscribed: .A. Celidonie (water of celandine)
Illustrated: *Antiques*, Feb., 1967, p. 204, fig. 7

89. DISH
Deruta (Umbria), *circa* 1515

White ground with design
in blue and light copper luster
9½" diameter

90. DISH with design of penitent St. Jerome
Deruta (Umbria), *circa* 1520

Lustered
15⅝" diameter
Ex collection Henry Nyburg, Aldbourne

91. DISH with design of St. Augustine

Deruta (Umbria), *circa* 1530–1540

13" diameter

Illustrated: Dr. J. Chompret, *Repertoire de la Majolica Italienne,* Paris, 1949, fig. 177, p. 25; *Antiques,* Feb. 1967, p. 204, fig. 6

Ex collections Fernandez; Whitney Warren, New York

92. DISH
Deruta (Umbria), *circa* 1515

Lustered
9⅝" diameter
Ex collection De Clemente

93. DISH
Venice, *circa* 1540

9⅝" diameter
Illustrated: Bernard Rackham,
Islamic Pottery and Italian Maiolica,
London, 1959, plate 212
Ex collections Imbert, Rome; Fernand Adda

94 A-B. PAIR OF ALBARELLI
Venice or Rome, late 16th century

9⅛" high
Inscribed: A: .X.A. in oval cartouche
E. D. BACIS .LAVRI (bayberry water)
B: .S.A. in oval cartouche; V. RASINI (grape wine)

95. DISH

Angarano (Veneto), early 18th century

10⅜" x 13⅛"
Relief molded
Cf. Bernard Rackham, *Catalogue of Italian Maiolica*, plate 191, No. 1194, where, after a discussion, a similar dish is attributed to Venice and, W. B. Honey, *European Ceramic Art from the End of the Middle Ages to About 1815*, Vol. I, London, 1949, where a dish with an identical border is attributed to Venice
Illustrated: *Antiques*, Feb. 1967, front cover

96. JUG
North Italy,
16th–17th century

5½" high

97. PILGRIM BOTTLE
North Italy, second half of 16th century

Cream-colored slip carved with color accents in brown and green
7" high
Ex collection J. H. Fitzhenry
Cf. *La Ceramica Graffata in Emilia-Romagna*, Modena, del Museo Civico, 1971, No. 249
Illustrated: *Antiques*, Feb., 1967, p. 204, fig. 5

98. **BARBER BOWL**
Castelli (Abruzzi),
mid-17th century

15″ long; 11¼″ greatest width
Possibly by Francesco Grue (1618–73)
The dust jacket shows this bowl
in actual size

99. DISH
Castelli (Abruzzi),
18th century

White ground with design in green, brown, orange, and blue
6¾" diameter

100. **ALBARELLO**
Castelli (Abruzzi), dated 1721

Bluish-white ground with design in blue, pale green, light and dark orange
4⅝" high
Inscribed: TERIACA. ROM (Theriaca Romanum)
Theriaca was originally an antidote against poisons, but eventually was regarded as a universal remedy. There were numerous varieties of Theriaca, some with as many as seventy-three ingredients, others with as few as four
Ex collection Theo C. Landon, Topeka, Kansas

101. ALBARELLO
South Italy, probably Laterza,
17th century

11" high

102-103. PAIR OF SALTS
Cerreto Sannita (Apulia),
18th century

White ground with decorations in yellow, blue, green, manganese, and orange
Each 7⅝" high

104. DRUG JAR
South Italy possibly Vietri,
18th century

White ground with design in blue
9⅝" high
Inscribed: VESTITO DA MINORE SENE
PASSA IN ASSISI A VISITARE I SVO
INTERCESSARE S. FRANCESCO

105. ALBARELLO with
Arms of the Knights of Malta
Caltagirone (Sicily),
circa 1722–1736

White ground with design in blue, green, yellow, and brown
13 1/6" high

The arms are the same as those on a set of large jars of which one is illustrated by Giuseppe Liverani, *Selezione delle Opere*, Faenza, 1963, No. 78, where the arms are identified as those of Antonio Manoel de Vilhena, a Portuguese, 66th grand master of the Order of Malta (1722–1736).

106. ALBARELLO with design of St. Peter Martyr
Palermo (Sicily), dated 1610

White ground with design in manganese, blue, orange, and yellow
10¼" high
Illustrated: *Antiques*, Feb. 1967, p. 206, fig. 13

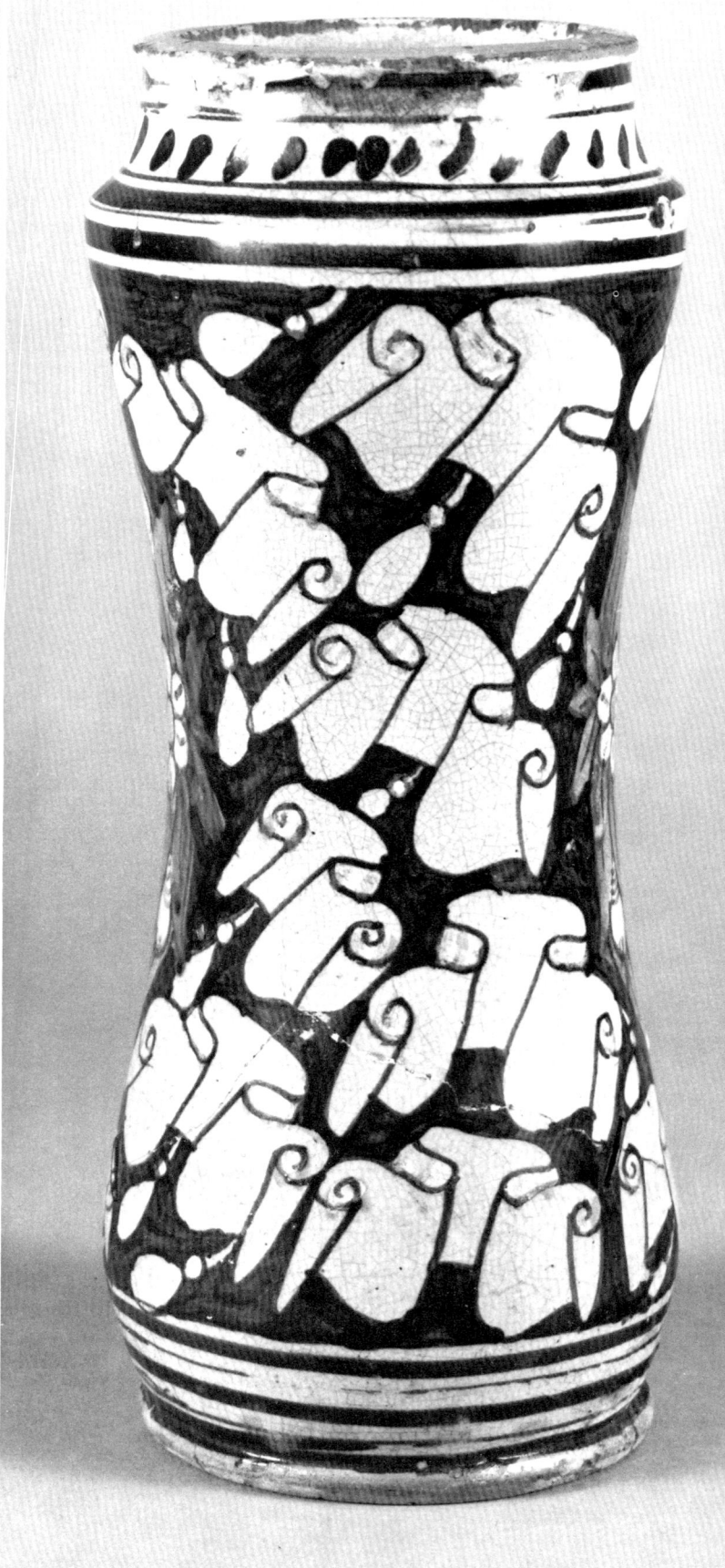

107. ALBARELLO
Trapani (Sicily), 17th century

White ground with design in blue, green, and yellow
11⅛" high
Illustrated: *Antiques*, Feb. 1967, p. 206, fig. 13

108. ALBARELLO
Trapani (Sicily), 17th century

White ground with design in blue, green, yellow, orange, and brown
10⅝" high

109. DISH with relief design of "Fecundity"

France, second half of 16th century

School of Bernard Palissy
Lead glaze
16¼" high x 19⅝" wide
Illustrated: Ross E. Taggart, *Burnap Collection of English Pottery*, revised edition 1967, p. 43
Cf. W. B. Honey, *European Ceramic Art from the End of the Middle Ages to About 1815*, Vol. I, London, 1949 at plate 20C and Robert J. Charleston, ed., *World Ceramics, An Illustrated History*, London, 1968, plate 350, p. 120

NORTHERN EUROPE

110. DISH
London (Lambeth), dated 1674

White ground with decorations in blue, green, yellow, and orange
16" high x 19¼" wide
English copy of the Palissy dish No. 109
Illustrated: Ross E. Taggart, *Relief Ornamented Ceramics*, Kansas City, 1963, plate 41, p. 28

111. DISH with relief designs of fish and reptiles

France, late 16th– early 17th century

School of Bernard Palissy
Lead glaze
8½" high x 12¾" wide

112. DISH
France, 16th–17th century

School of Bernard Palissy
Cream ground; center "tortoise shell" in brown with green; border green
Lead glaze
17" diameter
Ex collection Hinckle Smith, Philadelphia

113. MORTAR
Probably Avignon
17th century

Red-orange clay with lead glaze in the form of a 16th-century French bronze mortar
3½" high; 5¾" diameter

114. DISH with the Arms of the Second Duke of Hamilton
Moustiers (France), 18th century

White ground with design in orange, blue, brown, and green
9⅝" diameter

115. TILE in form of a Gothic niche
South Germany or Tirol;
Possibly Kärnten; 15th century

Green lead glaze
11⅛" x 7"
Ex collection Oscar Bundy, Vienna

116. TILE with relief of an angel
South Germany or Tirol,
late 15th–early 16th century
Yellow lead glaze
7⅞" x 6"
Ex collection Oscar Bundy, Vienna

117. JUG with spout in form of the head of a fanciful animal

South Germany: possibly Tirol; 15th–16th century

10½" greatest height
Ex collection Oscar Bundy, Vienna

118. RONDELL with relief of "The Annunciation"
South Germany; Nürenberg(?); late 15th–early 16th century

Lead glaze
12¾" diameter
Ex collection Oscar Bundy, Vienna

119. CISTERN with relief design
Rhenish or South Germany, dated 1592

Overall height 15¼"
Ex collections John Ribton Garstin, Braganstown; Castle Caldwell, Dublin
Inscribed: E. 1592 R (Elizabeth Regina)
Each side ornament with half of the design seen on the front

120. ALBARELLO 10⅛" high
Netherlands, Ex collection Edwin L. Weisl, New York
16th century

121. MOLDED DISH All white
Holland (?), late 17th century 12¾" diameter

122. BALASTER VASE
Holland (?), late 17th century

11½" high
Obverse with design of a standing Chinese man

123. SALT
Holland, 18th century

Blue-white ground, design in blue
4⅝" high

124. GROUP OF TILES
Probably Portugal, 17th century

15½" x 12¾"
Ex collection Dr. M. Hugo Oelze, Amsterdam
Inscribed: NA.SA. De Beln
"Our Lady of Belen" (Bethlehem)

Cf. *Carreaux Céramiques Hollandais Au Portugal et En Espagne* por J. M. Dos Santōs Ismóes De L'Académie Des Beaux–Arts De Lisbonne, 1959, where, at Plate VIIIb Dr. Ismóes illustrates a tile, with similar but more elaborate border tiles, depicting the death of Saint Thérèse, and attributes it to manufacture in Holland for the Portuguese market

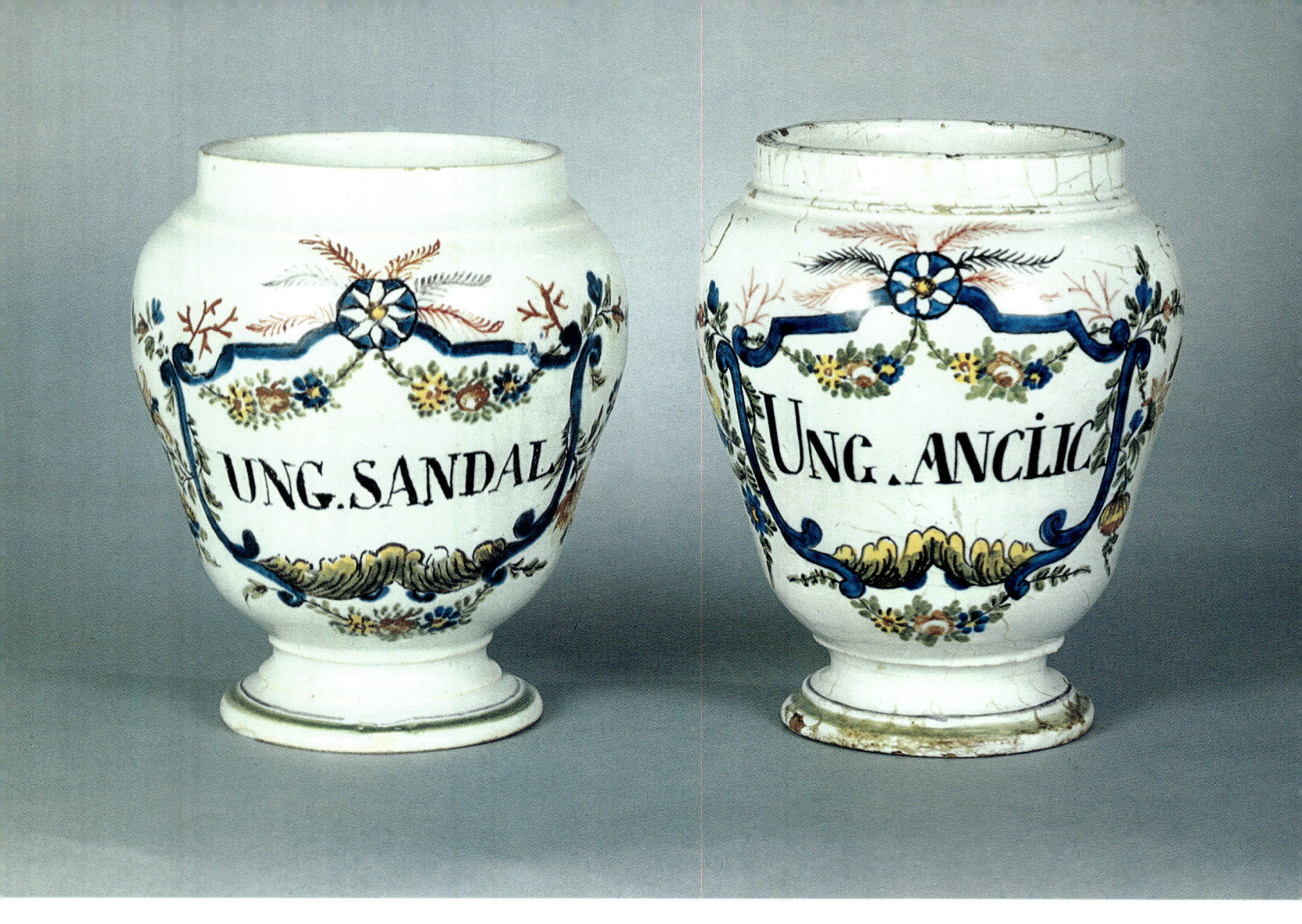

125. PAIR OF UNGUENT JARS

Lenzburg (Switzerland), 18th century

6¾" high and 7" high
Inscribed: UNG. SANDAL (sandalwood ointment)
UNG. ANGLIC (angelica ointment)

SELECTED BIBLIOGRAPHY

Atil, Esin. *Ceramics from the World of Islam*. (Fiftieth Anniversary Exhibition). Washington, D.C.: Freer Gallery of Art, 1973.

Barber, Edwin Atlee. *Catalogue of Mexican Maiolica Belonging to Mrs. Robert W. De Forest*. New York: The Hispanic Society of America, 1911.

Barber, Edwin Atlee. *The Emily Johnston De Forest Collection of Mexican Maiolica*. New York: The Metropolitan Museum of Art, 1918.

Caviro, Balbina Martinez. *Catalogo De Ceramica Espanola*. Madrid, 1968.

Caviro, Balbina Martinez. *Ceramica De Talavera*. Madrid, 1969.

Charleston, Robert J., ed. *World Ceramics, An Illustrated History*. London, 1968.

Chompret, Joseph. *Faiences Francaises Primitives* . . . Paris: Les Editions Nomis, 1946.

Chompret, Joseph. *Repertoire de la Majolica Italienne*. 2 vols. Paris: Les Editions Nomis, 1949.

Cirici, Alexandre. *Cerámica Catalana*. Barcelona, 1977.

Cora, Galeazzo. *Storia della Maiolica di Firenze e del Contado*. Florence, 1973.

Donatone, Guido. *Maioliche Napoletani della Speziera Aragonese di Castelnuovo*. Naples, 1970.

Drey, Rudolf E. A. *Apothecary Jars*. London & Boston: Faber and Faber, 1978.

Fehérvári, Géza. *Islamic Pottery* . . . *the Barlow Collection*. London: Faber and Faber Ltd., 1973.

Fortnum, Charles D. E. *Maiolica in the Ashmolean Museum*. Oxford, 1896.

Frothingham, Alice Wilson. *Catalogue of Hispano-Moresque Pottery in the Collection of the Hispanic Society of America*. New York, 1936.

Frothingham, Alice Wilson. *Lustreware of Spain*. New York: Hispanic Society of America, 1951.

Frothingham, Alice Wilson. *Talavera Pottery*. New York: Hispanic Society of America, 1944.

Frothingham, Alice Wilson. *Tile Panels of Spain 1500-1600*. New York, 1969.

Honey, William Bowyer. *European Ceramic Art from the End of the Middle Ages to About 1815*. Vol. 1, Illustrated Historical Survey. Vol. 2, A Dictionary . . . London: Faber and Faber Ltd., 1949-1952.

Honey, William Bowyer. *The Art of the Potter*. London: Faber and Faber, 1946.

Husband, Timothy. "Valencian Lusterware of the Fifteenth Century: Notes and Documents." *The Metropolitan Museum of Art Bulletin*, Summer, 1970.

Ismóes, J. M. Dos Santos. *Carreaux Céramiques Hollandais Au Portugal et En Espagne*, 1959.

Kassebaum, John Philip. "Italian Majolica: a Summary based on American Collection." *Antiques*, vol. XCI, no. 2, February, 1967.

Laboratorios del norte de Espana, S.A., Masnou, Barcelona (Sp.). Museo Retrospectivo de farmacia y medicina, 1952. Series: Laboratorios del norte de Espana, S.S., Masnou (Sp.). Publication, 180.

Lane, Arthur. *Early Islamic Pottery*. London: Faber and Faber, 1947.

Lane, Arthur. *Later Islamic Pottery*. London: Faber and Faber Ltd., 1957.

Lane, Arthur. Victoria and Albert Museum, *Guide to the Collection of Tiles*. London, 1939.

Liverani, Giuseppe. *Five Centuries of Italian Maiolica*. New York: McGraw Hill, 1960.

Liverani, Giuseppe. *Selezione delle Opere*. Faenza, 1963.

Mallet, John V. G. "Francesco Urbini in Gubbio and Deruta." *Bollettino del Museo Internazionale delle Ceramiche di Faenza* LXV, No. 6 (1979).

Mallet, John V. G. "Some Maiolicas from Faenza in English Collections." *Bollettino del Museo Internazionale Ceramiche di Faenza*, 1974.

Modena, Museo Civico. *La Ceramica Graffata in Emilia—Romagna*. Modena, 1971.

Batllori y Munné, A. and Llubia y Munné, L. M. *Ceramica Catalana Decorada*. Barcelona, 1974.

Passerini, Luigi. *Genealogia e Storia della Famiglia Corsini*. Firenze, 1858.

Pataky, Ilona (Brestyanszky). *Italienische Majolikakunst; italienische Majolika in ungarischen Sammlungen*. Budapest: Corvina, 1967.

Rackham, Bernard. *Catalogue of the Glaisher Collection of Pottery & Porcelain*, 2 vols. Cambridge: The University Press, 1935.

Rackham, Bernard. *Islamic Pottery and Italian Maiolica*. London: Faber and Faber, 1959.

Rackham, Bernard. *Italian Maiolica*. New York: Pitman Publishing Corporation [1952?].

Rackham, Bernard. Victoria and Albert Museum, *Catalogue of Italian Maiolica*. 2 vols. London, 1940.

Rackham, Bernard. Victoria and Albert Museum, *Catalogue of Italian Maiolica*. With emendations and additional bibliography by J. V. G. Mallet. 2 vols. London: Her Majesty's Stationery Office, 2nd impression, 1977.

Rackham, Bernard. Victoria and Albert Museum, *Guide to Italian Maiolica*. London, 1933.

Ridout, William. *A Catalogue of the Collection of Italian and Other Maiolica, Mediaeval English Pottery, Dutch, Spanish and French Faience, and other Ceramic Wares*. London, 1934.

San Francisco, California Palace of the Legion of Honor. *The Triumph of Humanism; Exhibition of the Decorative Arts of the Legion of Honor*. 1977.

Sauerlandt, von Max. *Das Museum Für Kunst und Gewerbe in Hamburg 1877-1927*. Hamburg, 1929.

Schottmuller, Frida. *Furniture and Interior Decoration of the Italian Renaissance*. New York: Brentano's, 1921.

Solon, M. L. *A History and Description of Italian Maiolica*. London: Cassell and Company, Ltd., 1907.

Taggart, Ross E. "Relief Ornamented Ceramics . . ." *The Nelson Gallery-Atkins Museum Bulletin*, vol. IV, no. 3. Kansas City, 1963.

Taggart, Ross E. *The Frank P. and Harriet C. Burnap Collection of English Pottery in the William Rockhill Nelson Gallery*. Kansas City, revised edition, 1967.

Vydrova, Jiřina. *Italian Majolica*. (Translated by Ota Vojtíšek.) London, 1960.

Walcher, Alfred. *Die Deutsche Keramic in Der Sammlung Figdor*. Wien, 1909.